BITTER SWEET

Bitter Sweet

ASIA HARRIS

Book Brush

Asia The Writer

AUTHOR BIO

Asia Harris is the author behind the illustrious anthology, Bitter Sweet and the urban fiction novel, Life's Rollercoaster. She is an artist, playwright, screenwriter, poet, author, and music composer. As a playwright, she has had stage readings at Chicago State University for the 10-minute play festival. Asia is also an MFA, graduate in the Chicago State University's Creative Writing program.

CONTENTS

STRANDED based on 2Pac Shakur's Dear Mama

This that…lyrical content vocalized over that jazz in the grass

"Sadie you know I love you," type of beat

That "Mama Understand Me" hard headed adolescent type of story

That "Herbie baby, Herbie baby," V103 type of tempo

Tear's turns to lyrics

Indulging spirits

Hazy days;

Mom's nodding, "Yo mama's on crack rock," but I love her

"Parents just don't understand," feeling stranded

Pop's played Whodini

Now you see me now you don't

Resignation without notice

Burgundy colored cement

More chalk lines than chalk boards

Welfare raised in warfare

Caged, zoo kept;

Howling

confinement

Cuffs no links, the first custom jewelry accompanied.

Discoloration of wrists strangled by metal bracelets

Dodge balling bullets

Magazines full no images

Cold sweats from flashbacks

When it rains it pours

Shell casings on the floor

Black Panther movement

Saxophone kind of soothing

Living on borrowed time

Inhale waiting to exhale; ease the mind

Peanut butter sandwich for dinner

Street raised, another X…

marks the spot

Black ink branded

Love & respect moms, still stranded

LOVE RUSH

As we fuse like a daiquiri

Blissful explosion, so vibrant, so lyrical

coerced theatrical rush, ritual seemingly cynical.

Disappear in my sentiment of our ecstasy

Overdosing off of our chemicals, tangled in our web of a fairytale

FRIEND OR FOE
in remembrance of Kenneka Jenkins

In my city kids are chastised, then buried alive

Three plus three, they're clutched; or judged by twelve; the streets is the welcome guide, to glide

chalk lines replace hop scotch numbers, stretched, toe tags all summer.

They don't fight they duck-duck goose, in this call of duty display

Strange fruit is hanging, on live, viral

Co-stars in this new nightmare, produced by news channels,

sponsored by combat on Ishare. Poverty surrounded property

Ice sculpted, pain inflicted retaliation, "friendemies"

These streets are infected like a virus

Vigil's held for onyx colored jewels, drowning in a pool...

Blood baths, marketed like a craft, no beer; money flashing in the cam

Most likely to succeed another unsolved mystery

Parlors packed like 31, flavors, familiar flavors, one less kid on the school bus

to succeed got to hate to love the city where I'm from.

SAVE ME

Catch me

Before

I

drown.

PURE BLISS

Dismantle my identity until I am,
bare, as the sheets that envelop my virtuosity
His lips & hands survey my body
like a lesson he yearns to learn & teach.
Somehow our lips intertwine. Clawing his backside, we straddle;

Torturing my rose pedal, he traces the way;
tickling my juice box, devouring my saccharine,
Vicky is no longer a secret.
Silk between my toes as I arch my back
Fighting to be liberated, like I am under attack,
Mouth full of my bliss, his handle disappears
Then reappears…on repeat

A cry of liberation,
Strangled, muzzled by this craving.
Matching thrust to thrust, every angle
This is everything!

UNRECOGNIZED HERO in loving memory of my Grandma Edna B.

Checker board house coat, Daniel Greens that your pigeon toes rest in,
Sam doing his thing.
Hands on your hips, back bone slips, as the pots hum & sing.
Food for the soul…soul train to the nose,
Collards, Mac & cheese, sweets, & cornbread… oh so moist.
Food so good make you wanna slap your mama,
Um, um, um…
Food porn.
Decks being shuffled, misdeals causing trouble,
Dominoes pimp slapping the table.
Beer bottles click clacked in the trash,
Have to defrost the room from the cloudy airway,
Designer scents lingers whenever you made way.
You raised seven kids in addition to your grand kids,
"It takes a village," you said so you helped guide my friends,
"Be a little lady", always replays in my head.
On holidays I remember hearing the echo of the mixer, blending the cake batter,
I stayed in the kitchen just to lick the bowl,
Whenever you cooked you used your heart & soul!
You had me more spoiled than milk.
I can still feel the sizzle to my ear.
Still smell the burning of my hair,
You even added curls,

Had me looking like, "Just for me"
I trailed along like a carbon copy
You use to say, "You make me feel one hundred feet tall"
I smiled ear to ear whenever you said that to me.
You would splurge your last, a Christmas tree just for me,
Lights brighter than the eclipse, when we would decorate the tree,
Backbone of the family;
Big Mama of the house, my hero, my pride & joy, I love you
Grandma BB

HELLO SUMMER

Bud Billiken Parade
Air & water show
Crap games, dogs barking
Freshly manicured, car shows
Adding pounds at the Taste...
Lollapalooza festival multitude
Cook out vapors, firework sparks,
melodic chimes, as the ice cream truck ride by.

Red paint, identical to the tape...
Flickering, red alarms.
sirens high-pitched,
birds whistling.

Sun beaming,
you're it; better go hide & go seek,
before you're left holey, like Swiss,
cheese; say cheese.... another mug shot.
"One, two, Freddy's coming for you,"
Nightmares are the new reality.
Unfulfilled dreams.

EXPIRATION

Life ain't

promised

death

is

DEATH & DEMONS written by a 10-year-old me

The demons are chasing me,

in my dreams I'm trying to get away...

I'm running and screaming trying not to get caught,

maybe it'll help if I pray.

If I pray will that help? It can't hurt to try...

Please Lord don't let me get caught;

I'm not ready to die

UNCONDITIONAL

Love

Interlock

Compassion

Patience

Trust

Faith

Together

Us

MY BLACK IS BEAUTIFUL

Color out of style

brown boys like a throwaway

black beauty a fad

GO WITH THE FLOW

Charged like a cable

Lit candles, wine, and sweet sounds

Painful bliss no rules

JULY

Eyes squinting, beaming lights...
Like Parkinson's, the wind shakes,
It softly kisses my cheek.
feeling fluttered.
Trees sway like a slow dance,
Kids play like they last chance...
Could it be?

Grills blazing on the lake while the water bops,
earsplitting harmony.
Sirens roar...
Miss Mary Mack all dressed in black...
You hear no more...

Faces & memories plastered on t-shirts.
Churches overloaded with chocolate covered desserts,
Zip locked beings,
Hollow tips soaring...
Sharp screams are deafening

Luminous fireworks pierce the sky for the fourth of July
Skittle colored sparks
Young boys on the corners turn's to tumblers & drummers
Fumes of herbal essence linger.
Life as I know it, life in the Chi...

Welcome home July

UNIVERSAL LOVE

In my city children are buried alive, already

afraid to sleep, dreams are haunting, I

hear sirens every night, am…

I, inferior to the naked eye? No

hopes, dreams scattered, oppression is lasting even longer

Does my life matter? Looked

upon as a soiled, sinister being, at

the dream of King and our ancestors is obsolete, with

infectious beings seemingly purity, lechery

is only for the onyx jewels, or

is everything good reserved for the so-called privileged, love

is universal.

I CAN'T BREATHE

Mutiny, & racial patterns
Causes a lapse in dreams as they begin to scatter
Pain overpowers the laughter
The game is molded like plaster
Our culture is no disaster
Placing us on a platter...
As if we do not matter
Black lives Matter...

We need to launch justice and peace
In this world full of power & greed
Expecting us to remain quietly
They say we are free
In this masked society
Yet they try to remix our history

Attempting to trap our culture like a prison
& devoid our mission
We are trapped in a world that's ran by those with minds stuck in
slavery
Still we are fighting like Rosa
Speaking our truth like Ida with dreams big as King
All lives matter...everyone deserves equivalent opportunities

As we strive for conformity & unity

To complete our destiny & release our tormented history
This unmerited treatment is affecting you, you & me
Black lives matter…. I can't Breathe…

MAYBE....

Maybe I write because Martin had a dream
Because Frederick broke free...
Maybe I write because Trayvon, Nipsey & Pac received their
wings, early
Maybe I write because of Sojourner's truth
Onyx colored gems gazed like leftover stew

Maybe I write because Rosa fought to end segregation
& because of the countless racist sanctions

Maybe I write because it's a strange world we living...
slaughtered for so called whistling
The injustice of Emmitt's lynching
Jealousy & envy.... blood is trickling
Maybe I write because of this agonizing history revisiting

Maybe I write for the black aesthetic
Maybe I write to release my pain to the tablet
Maybe I write because of cultural classics
Such as Pat Smith, August Wilson, & Gwen Brooks
Maybe I write so my words are ingested like it's been cooked

Maybe I write to inscribe my reality
Maybe I write to end police brutality

Maybe I write for the lost souls… who haven't a clue
Maybe I write as a way to capture you

Maybe I write because of my, "shade impairment"
Maybe I write because it's relevant
Maybe I write for abolitionist like Ida
Maybe I write because my ancestors were looked at like vipers
Maybe I write because African American mores, is the flame to a lighter

Maybe I write because I am tenacious like X
Maybe I write to rupture barriers through text
Maybe I write because our ancestors fought for you, they fought for me
Maybe I write as a form of existence of my very being

Maybe I write because our story keeps shifting
Maybe I write to paint a picture so vivid

Maybe I write because my words are my tears
Maybe I write for my peers
Maybe I write to overcome my fears

Maybe I write for feminist power
Maybe I write so my culture won't devour
Maybe I write for African folklore
Maybe I write so my heart can pour

Maybe I write because music is my 1st love
Maybe I write as a dose of medicine strong as cod liver oil
Maybe I write because I know what it's like to sleep on the floor
Maybe I write as a declaration of my core
Maybe I write as a trinket that I exist
Maybe I write as a survival kit

Maybe I write so my bruises will fade
Maybe I write for past memories of the fallen angels in the grave
Maybe I write because I am content with my shade
Maybe I write so my tale will be saved

Maybe I write because I am the voice of the misunderstood
Maybe I write because by verse I am prolific & I'm doing what I
should

Maybe I write because of the influence that my grandma had
Maybe I write because I was raised a single mom without my dad
Maybe I write because some of this love be so fake
Maybe I write to release some of my hurt I keep stored away

Maybe I write because I remember Marvin's voice whispering to me
Maybe I write because I saw my cousin's body, lifeless, like one out
of a movie scene
Maybe I write because I have lost so many to these streets
Maybe I write because I found my uncle OD'D
Maybe I write because the story that I am painting is what you
need to see

LOGGING OFF

Anxiously waiting for my heart to awaken.
Out of order & forsaken…
Mending the tiny pieces that's been breaking.
Abrasions that won't heal…
Old flames stay lit.
From every direction, my hearts been hit
Your presence entered into my life, taught me to brag different

Your authenticity,
unified with our chemistry,
makes me feel, free inside.
It's that unexplainable feeling
That makes life worth living.
Now I see why it didn't work out with others in the beginning.

No longer riding a rollercoaster
I have a burning desire…
Only you can ignite my fire

Our dynasty is strong…
I hear our story in those mushy love songs
Didn't think real love was possible until you came along

Our love will never mold

Our story is too bold
I see you everywhere I go
I never want you to let me go

Our unity is preserved
Hash tag relationship goals, It's finally my turn

To my puzzle, you are the missing piece…
I'm logging off now, my search is over, I'm complete

FROM WITHIN

As my tears strike the page with thoughts that has been bottled inside If I told you my life story you would question how I survived I grasp for air as I release my agony the words that chime from within my spine are all my cries as I erase some lines as my story rewinds unsure of my fate trapped inside like enduring hard times I am no longer victimized as I visualize my success no longer am I institutionalized & hindered as I attempt to free my spirit utilizing my gift of voice & reasoning no longer a burden as I bloom like a tainted flower I let my words linger realizing I am the tone of the misunderstood it is I who leads the blind I am legendary I am filled with life as grace & mercy protects me while the devil tries to overpower me nudging the old me I am empowered as I walk with faith to complete my destiny.

GAME OVER

No longer am I accepting resumes to fill the void, my heart is
vacant...
Trust issues keep me distant, never to be complacent
He loves me, he loves me not, I'm over it now... tangled
Grasping for air as I feel strangled
Real devotion is translucent instead I am blinded by every angle
Not sure how we became so mangled

Yet & still I yearn for a love so authentic, I'm still full of hope
Should I leave or should I stay? I block list your number as I
attempt to cope
You try to be slick, but the games you play, I scope

Some actions don't require a response, I stay muted though
Our love seems diluted, yet I'm your so-called preference
Premium chick not unleaded, yet your goods is on clearance

It's like you're here, then you gone, then you're here, then you
gone, then you're here...
Then...poof... another disappearance
You say, "Teach me how to love", yet you feel you are undeserving
of admiration, so you flee
Always an option in your life instead of being a priority
I'm so exhausted, by your very being
Tired of trying...if it's real it should flow naturally

counterfeit promises constantly.

Your immaturity is making my heart grow colder & colder
so, bundle up, I'm not settling.
I want it all…
Game over

MY HERO

When I was a caterpillar, I wore baby doll clothes,
my
Pops use to sing to me, "I just called to say I love you", the
love
seemed so official. I was opaque, nursed by moms. He
was
as cool as the winters breeze...I love when
my
hero...he would sing to me. My
daddy
was a rolling stone, like he is from Vegas, he seemed life-size to me
he
appeared big, until he became small, he
was
as smooth as a baby's bottom,
my
daddy drifted on a memory, face was left on a milk carton. My
hero
trained in disappearing like a specialty. His time was no longer
spent with me
he
seemingly didn't choose me, all that mattered since the divorce
was his other family. I
was
not important to him anymore or, ever was I?
my
daddy would have me eager to go play with my siblings. At
first

I would pack my bag, impatiently waiting as hours passed. Guess he didn't
love
me the way he did his other family

MISPLACED FREEDOM

Colored… like one out of a crayon box
Reddened as my flesh is scorching hot
Operational, in a plantation until my hands turn red & blue
calluses on my palms as I continue living this blues

Come across as hazardous waste,
based on my gender & race
Ethnocentricity still exist, still I am part of this race
& I race & I race & I race & I…race

Until my feet are bloody & freedom rings
back containing lashes
pride enclose permanent gashes
so many of ours dumped like ashes
breaking out like rashes
my freedom is misplaced

IS IT ENOUGH?

Over analyzing this condition, makes me wonder about us…
Am I an equal entity or am I just a tint to your shadow
Can this union, weather the storm?
Scars still throb, from ruptured pieces that's been torn…

They say love is enough, but really is it?
Are you a real one or is forever some sort of taboo?
Will this crumble, like my last hair do?
Or will it withstand the rain & be a debut to an, "I DO"

Answer me this, is there really an us?
Or better yet tell me this, was there ever an us?
I rocked with you since you were a pup
Believing in us, still & all like Nintendo you switch up

Stayed down all ten toes in it
Motivating you like your personal trainer
It's saddening something so real can end up as perfect strangers
Can't shake…the inevitable
Is our story real, or is it a fable?
Soaring as my heart skips another beat, as it feels dangled
As we are labeled a label
All I can think is, was this a mirage…is it enough?

LYRICAL ECSTASY

Seducing my mind as my soul explodes
Prada lingers through the airways as it slowly seeps through my nose
Screaming out in ecstasy as your conversation pleasures me
The gaze in your eyes made me know you will devour me
Your warm breath on my neck makes me feel so heavenly

Your touch is never abrasive even when it's abrasive
A perfect mixture, like a manicured Picasso painting
Panting & waiting…
with high expectations
The perfect lyric to my favorite beat

FULLY LOADED

Threatened by us, scholars
They try to forbid us from knowledge
They want us to be illiterate, lacking that, Black Panther power
Only a coward would remain mute & allow such immoral actions
As our "free" city attempts to split our melanin, like fractions
Forcing us to work twice as hard ...twice as hard we work
& we work & we work & we work...& we...work
Till our bones hurt

Still we will, never be good enough
In order to obtain our dignity, we created the Black Arts Movement
Labeled as, "Colored" so is other ethnicities considered discolored?
They want us muzzled

As we are born, "free" with more strikes than a bowling pin
They want us uniformed containing more stripes than zebra prints
Brutalized, malnourished & mutilated
Facts flowing no defamation
Our flaws are magnified
yet our scuffles are written in fine print
We're full of innovative spirits
But we are treated like loaded clips

They want to rewrite our narration
Where were you when our ancestors picked more cotton than

candy?
Laboring till they bled out & if the ran the cost would be deadly

Hung like wet clothes
In the field humming Negro spirituals
Innocence stolen by the oppressing bandit

Lifeless bodies stacking on ships like Jenga pieces
Chained & whipped like animals for whatever reason
Living our blues surrounded reality like an August Wilson script
We are remaining fully loaded

FADED

Ashes to ashes, dust to dust
Lost souls wither away, eyes wide shut
Cranberry color stains… they paint the scene
Puncture holes to the jugular
Donut hole to the brain
shoes & clothes drenched, same as cranberry stains
Teddy bears, flowers & RIP Tees
Bagged & tagged, more holes than they truth

Last thing recalled is, "License & registration, yes I'm talking to you"
Casualties of war
Obstructing justice they say we were snagged for
Lesions from these heathens
Breathless…
They hate to see us breathing
faded

WHEN MY TIME COME

Written by a 16-year old me in loving memory of David "Drilla" Hutchinson

When my time come the world gone be sick
Rushing me to my casket, knowing while they were blasting, I was laughing
Yeah... that was funny to me
If them haters didn't have mag, they'd be running from me
Damn, this the first time without my strap
guess it'll be my last
Because the hater with the mask sent me to the past
But it ain't shit cause now it's going down
One day they'll be bagged & placed in the ground

Never thought it'll be me catching rounds in my home town
Whoever bought that new Oozie that's that clown who sprayed me down
I knew it was you, cause' you was hating every time I came around
I prayed & now I found, what was above the cloud
You hear that sound?
That's the falling of my crown...
Now that I'm gone let my throne be my zone
Never ride out alone
Keep a, "chrome" or be prepared to hear that sad song
Cause until you gone, shit, it's on!

CASUALTIES OF WAR

The streets acting out like movie scenes

All I see is R.I.P. in my news feed

Bloodshed for misplaced anger & greed

Another tainted seed

Before they time, kids leave

Permanently...

This world is arctic...bitter & sweet

Can't out run these streets

They run to eternity

INTOXICATION

In a drunken state…
from the overbearing feeling you just can't shake.
Encompassing typhoons while the heart is one of the same
Staggering, from the intoxication
Bitter, sweet… atonement
Survival of these rocky moments
Mistakes chose to own it
Melodies describes your every moment
Riding the wave
Driving with no power steering
Indescribable feeling that brings you out of your shell
A love so phenomenal, intoxicated by the spell

PEACE BE STILL

As the water strikes my heaving chest

The depravities of yesterday are no more

The weight of the world is no longer an anchor

Joy cometh in the morning

I AM....

Louder than a bomb
I am…
the strength of Psalms
I am…
Uncensored like your favorite rap CD
I am…
fearless like Ida, who many wish they could be
I am…
The voice of my ancestors, who paved the way
I am…
A web of poetry, & the pain of the enslaved
I am…
A celebration like Clifton
I am…
Perfectly unperfected
I am…who I am…
I am…Still standing

MOTHER'S LOVE

Selflessly, you've been here for me
Carried me in your womb
Pray for me when my life seems rugged
Shoving me towards greatness, when my vision seems blurry
Believing in my dreams, even when it seems far away
Grip my hand, to keep me going, when you feel me slipping away

Your belief, helps me believe
In myself, in my dreams
Former tainted seed, blossoming, with leaves
You love me through my highs & my lows…
Front row to my shows

Did what you could, with no regrets
Give your last to me, never seen you sweat

To you I bow
love you always, your only child
I vow to make you proud